Magic Eye 3-D Optical Illusion Cards: Hold this postcard *right up to your nose* and *very very slowly* pull it away from your face. Look *through* the image without focusing on it. Try not to blink, and a hidden image will magically appear!

© 1994 N.E. Thing Enterprises

Andrews and McMeel, Kansas City, MO 64112

Hidden Image: Surfer

Magic Eye 3-D Optical Illusion Cards: Hold this postcard *right up to your nose* and *very very slowly* pull it away from your face. Look *through* the image without focusing on it. Try not to blink, and a hidden image will magically appear!

© 1994 N.E. Thing Enterprises

Andrews and McMeel, Kansas City, MO 64112

Hidden Image: 3 fish

Magic Eye 3-D Optical Illusion Cards: Hold this postcard *right up to your nose* and *very very slowly* pull it away from your face. Look *through* the image without focusing on it. Try not to blink, and a hidden image will magically appear!

© 1994 N.E. Thing Enterprises

Andrews and McMeel, Kansas City, MO 64112

Hidden Image: "LOVE" and Iris flowers

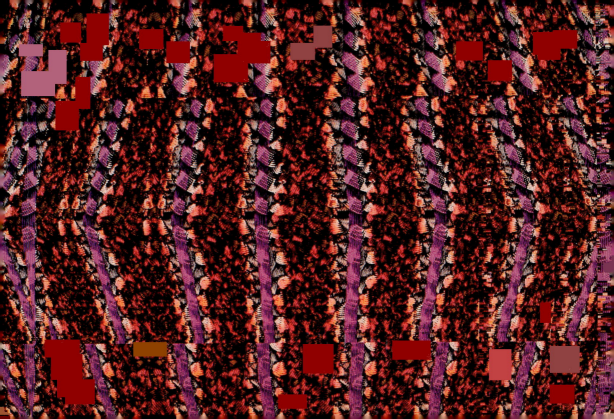

Magic Eye 3-D Optical Illusion Cards: Hold this postcard *right up to your nose* and *very very slowly* pull it away from your face. Look *through* the image without focusing on it. Try not to blink, and a hidden image will magically appear!

© 1994 N.E. Thing Enterprises

Andrews and McMeel, Kansas City, MO 64112

Hidden Image: Dimensional perspective squares

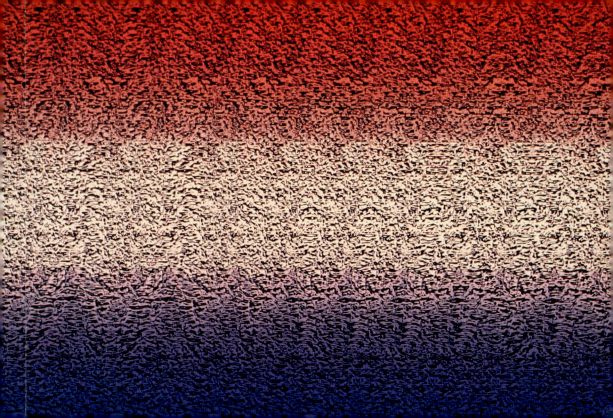

Magic Eye 3-D Optical Illusion Cards: Hold this postcard *right up to your nose* and *very very slowly* pull it away from your face. Look *through* the image without focusing on it. Try not to blink, and a hidden image will magically appear!

Andrews and McMeel, Kansas City, MO 64112

Hidden Image: Liberty bell

Place stamp here

Magic Eye 3-D Optical Illusion Cards: Hold this postcard *right up to your nose* and *very very slowly* pull it away from your face. Look *through* the image without focusing on it. Try not to blink, and a hidden image will magically appear!

Place stamp here

Andrews and McMeel, Kansas City, MO 64112

Hidden Image: Clock

Magic Eye 3-D Optical Illusion Cards: Hold this postcard *right up to your nose* and *very very slowly* pull it away from your face. Look *through* the image without focusing on it. Try not to blink, and a 3-D illusion will magically appear!

Andrews and McMeel, Kansas City, MO 64112

Hidden Image: Dimensional Image

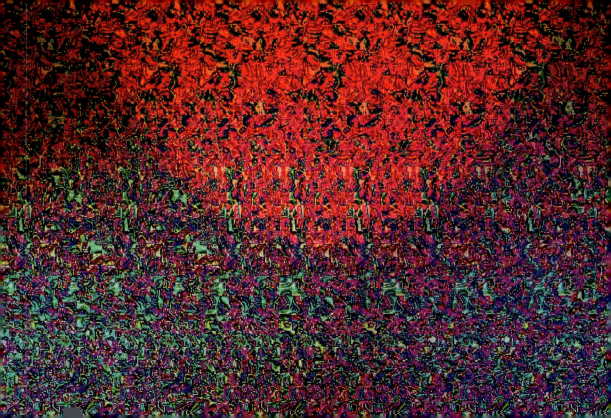

Magic Eye 3-D Optical Illusion Cards: Hold this postcard *right up to your nose* and *very very slowly* pull it away from your face. Look *through* the image without focusing on it. Try not to blink, and a hidden image will magically appear!

© 1994 N.E. Thing Enterprises

Andrews and McMeel, Kansas City, MO 64112

Hidden Image: Rocking horse

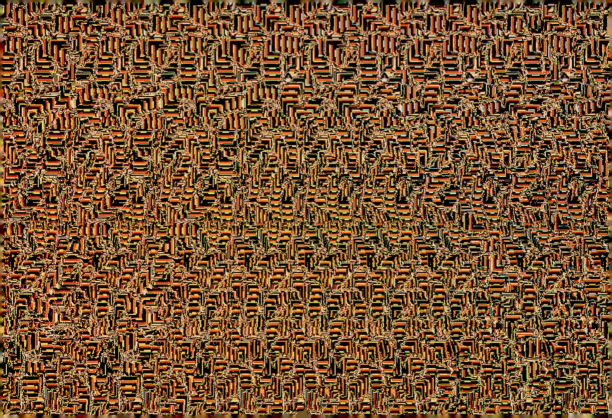

Magic Eye 3-D Optical Illusion Cards: Hold this postcard *right up to your nose* and *very very slowly* pull it away from your face. Look *through* the image without focusing on it. Try not to blink, and a hidden image will magically appear!

© 1994 N.E. Thing Enterprises

Place stamp here

Andrews and McMeel, Kansas City, MO 64112

Hidden Image: 3 monsters

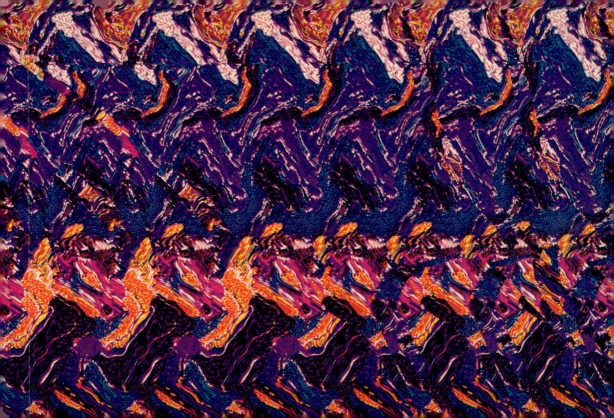

Magic Eye 3-D Optical Illusion Cards: Hold this postcard *right up to your nose* and *very very slowly* pull it away from your face. Look *through* the image without focusing on it. Try not to blink, and a hidden image will magically appear!

Place stamp here

Andrews and McMeel, Kansas City, MO 64112

Hidden Image: Spaceship

Magic Eye 3-D Optical Illusion Cards: Hold this postcard *right up to your nose* and *very very slowly* pull it away from your face. Look *through* the image without focusing on it. Try not to blink, and a hidden image will magically appear!

Place stamp here

Andrews and McMeel, Kansas City, MO 64112

Hidden Image: 2 hot air balloons

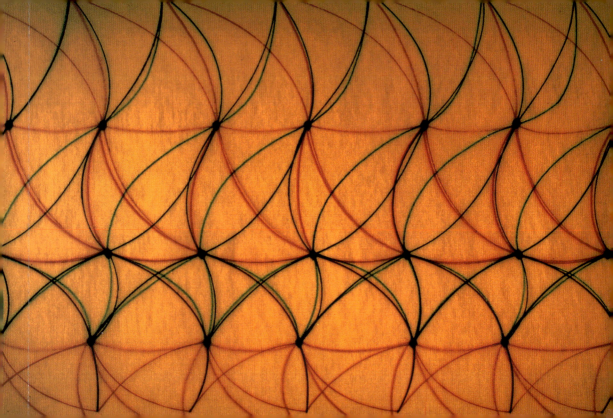

Magic Eye 3-D Optical Illusion Cards: Hold this postcard *right up to your nose* and *very very slowly* pull it away from your face. Look *through* the image without focusing on it. Try not to blink, and a 3-D illusion will magically appear!

Andrews and McMeel, Kansas City, MO 64112

Hidden Image: Dimensional Image

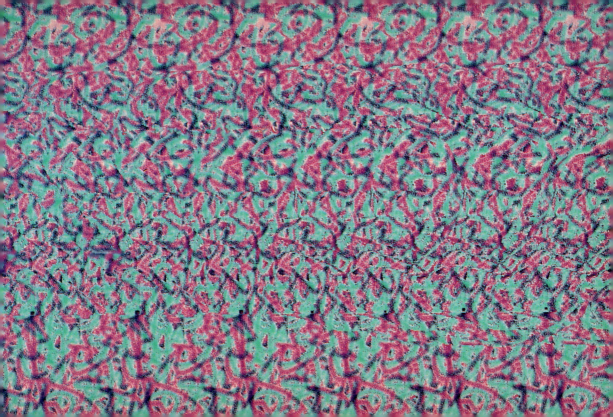

Magic Eye 3-D Optical Illusion Cards: Hold this postcard *right up to your nose* and *very very slowly* pull it away from your face. Look *through* the image without focusing on it. Try not to blink, and a hidden image will magically appear!

Andrews and McMeel, Kansas City, MO 64112

Hidden image: Hand holding a ball

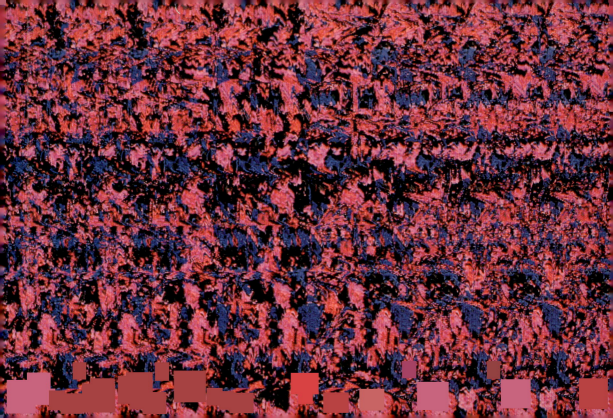

Magic Eye 3-D Optical Illusion Cards: Hold this postcard
right up to your nose and *very very slowly* pull it away from your
face. Look *through* the image without focusing on it. Try not to
blink, and a hidden image will magically appear!

Andrews and McMeel, Kansas City, MO 64112

Hidden Image: Cube with balls

Magic Eye 3-D Optical Illusion Cards: Hold this postcard *right up to your nose* and *very very slowly* pull it away from your face. Look *through* the image without focusing on it. Try not to blink, and a hidden image will magically appear!

© 1994 N.E. Thing Enterprises

Andrews and McMeel, Kansas City, MO 64112

Hidden Image: Deer (buck) head

Magic Eye 3-D Optical Illusion Cards: Hold this postcard
right up to your nose and *very very slowly* pull it away from your
face. Look *through* the image without focusing on it. Try not to
blink, and a hidden image will magically appear!

Place
stamp
here

Andrews and McMeel, Kansas City, MO 64112

Hidden Image: Basket weave pattern

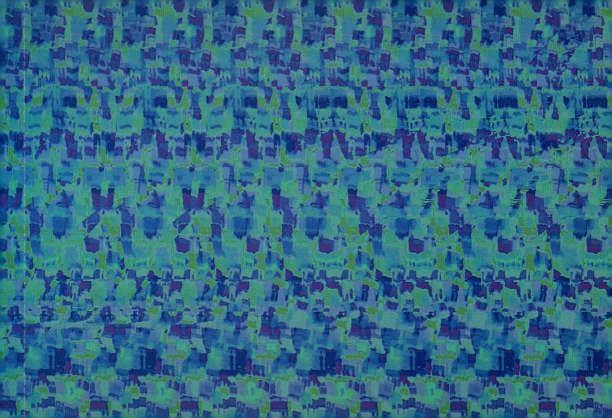

Magic Eye 3-D Optical Illusion Cards: Hold this postcard *right up to your nose* and *very very slowly* pull it away from your face. Look *through* the image without focusing on it. Try not to blink, and a hidden image will magically appear!

© 1994 N.E. Thing Enterprises

Andrews and McMeel, Kansas City, MO 64112

Hidden Image: Hammerhead shark

Magic Eye 3-D Optical Illusion Cards: Hold this postcard *right up to your nose* and *very very slowly* pull it away from your face. Look *through* the image without focusing on it. Try not to blink, and a hidden image will magically appear!

Andrews and McMeel, Kansas City, MO 64112

Hidden Image: Easter Island statues

Magic Eye 3-D Optical Illusion Cards: Hold this postcard *right up to your nose* and *very very slowly* pull it away from your face. Look *through* the image without focusing on it. Try not to blink, and a hidden image will magically appear!

Andrews and McMeel, Kansas City, MO 64112

Hidden Image: Wind-up drummer toys

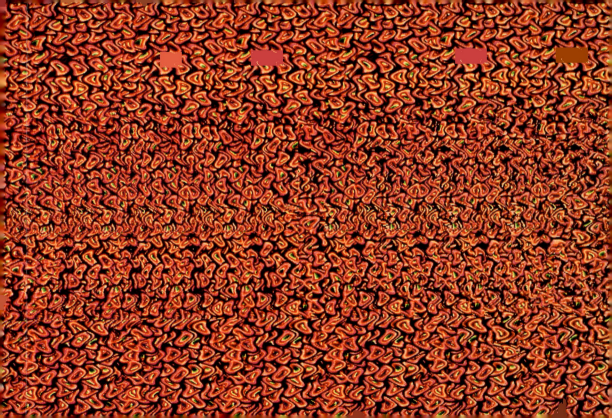

Magic Eye 3-D Optical Illusion Cards: Hold this postcard *right up to your nose* and *very very slowly* pull it away from your face. Look *through* the image without focusing on it. Try not to blink, and a hidden image will magically appear!

© 1994 N.E. Thing Enterprises

Andrews and McMeel, Kansas City, MO 64112

Hidden Image: 2 floating star cubes

Magic Eye 3-D Optical Illusion Cards: Hold this postcard *right up to your nose* and *very very slowly* pull it away from your face. Look *through* the image without focusing on it. Try not to blink, and a hidden image will magically appear!

Place stamp here

Andrews and McMeel, Kansas City, MO 64112

Hidden Image: Snake in a basket

Magic Eye 3-D Optical Illusion Cards: Hold this postcard *right up to your nose* and *very very slowly* pull it away from your face. Look *through* the image without focusing on it. Try not to blink, and a hidden image will magically appear!

Place stamp here

Andrews and McMeel, Kansas City, MO 64112

Hidden Image: 8 jacks

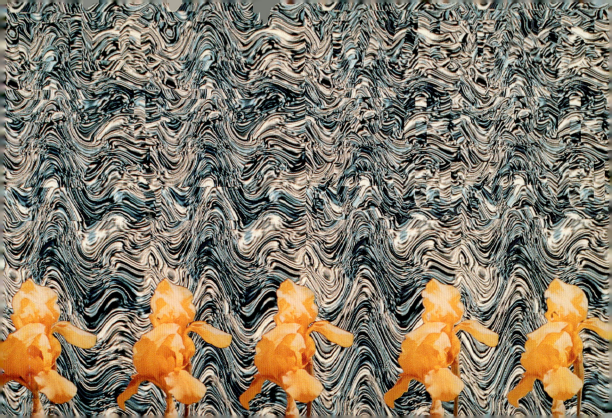

Magic Eye 3-D Optical Illusion Cards: Hold this postcard
right up to your nose and *very very slowly* pull it away from your
face. Look *through* the image without focusing on it. Try not to
blink, and a hidden image will magically appear!

Andrews and McMeel, Kansas City, MO 64112

Hidden Image: "FLOWERS FOR YOU."

© 1994 N.E. Thing Enterprises

Place stamp here

Andrews and McMeel, Kansas City, MO 64112

Hidden Image: Hooked on you

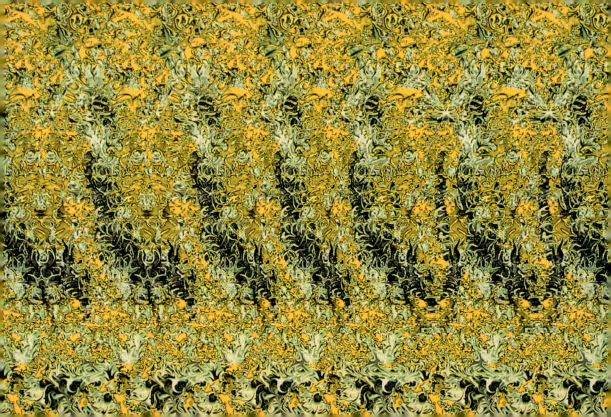

Magic Eye 3-D Optical Illusion Cards: Hold this postcard *right up to your nose* and *very very slowly* pull it away from your face. Look *through* the image without focusing on it. Try not to blink, and a hidden image will magically appear!

Andrews and McMeel, Kansas City, MO 64112

Hidden image: A face

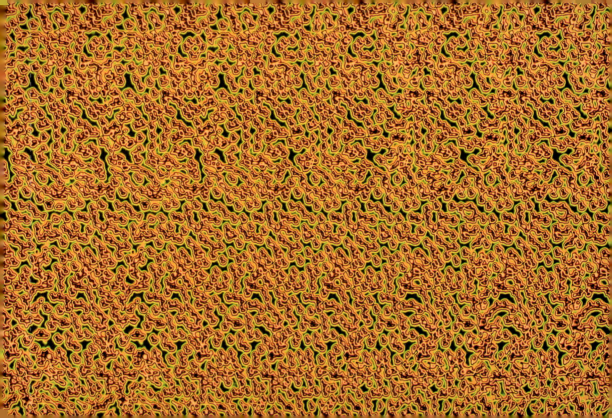

Magic Eye 3-D Optical Illusion Cards: Hold this postcard *right up to your nose* and *very very slowly* pull it away from your face. Look *through* the image without focusing on it. Try not to blink, and a hidden image will magically appear!

Andrews and McMeel, Kansas City, MO 64112

Hidden image: Buddha

Magic Eye 3-D Optical Illusion Cards: Hold this postcard *right up to your nose* and *very very slowly* pull it away from your face. Look *through* the image without focusing on it. Try not to blink, and a hidden image will magically appear!

Andrews and McMeel, Kansas City, MO 64112

Hidden image: Weird machine

Place stamp here

Magic Eye 3-D Optical Illusion Cards: Hold this postcard *right up to your nose* and *very very slowly* pull it away from your face. Look *through* the image without focusing on it. Try not to blink, and a hidden image will magically appear!

© 1994 N.E. Thing Enterprises

Andrews and McMeel, Kansas City, MO 64112

Hidden Image: Couple embracing

Magic Eye 3-D Optical Illusion Cards: Hold this postcard
right up to your nose and *very very slowly* pull it away from your
face. Look *through* the image without focusing on it. Try not to
blink, and a hidden image will magically appear!

Andrews and McMeel, Kansas City, MO 64112

Hidden image: Twisted coil